scribble, squiggle & sketch

by Kristi Thom

**75 easy-to-draw doodles
to decorate stickers, gift bags,
picture frames, and more!**

★ American Girl®

Published by American Girl Publishing
Copyright © 2012 by American Girl

Questions or comments? Call 1-800-845-0005,
visit **americangirl.com**, or write to Customer Service,
American Girl, 8400 Fairway Place, Middleton, WI 53562-0497.

Printed in China
13 14 15 16 17 18 LEO 10 9 8 7 6 5 4 3 2

All American Girl marks are trademarks of American Girl.

Editorial Development: Mary Richards Beaumont
Design: Gretchen Becker
Production: Jeannette Bailey, Sarah Boecher, Tami Kepler, Judith Lary, Jolene Schulz
Tabletop Photography: Jeff Rockwell

Photography: p. 4—© iStockphoto/Crisma (markers); p. 4—© iStockphoto/ bluestocking (pencil); p. 4—© iStockphoto/stockcam (paper); p. 5—© iStockphoto/ BrianAJackson (magnifying glass)

Dear Budding Artist,

Whether you already love to draw or are just starting out, there is something in this book for you. By following the steps, you'll learn to doodle animals, food, shoes, bugs, flowers—even a garden gnome! Once you learn how, you can use your doodles to decorate posters, bookmarks, cards, and more.

But we hope that you don't stop there. Once you discover how delightful doodling can be, try making up some doodles. Or even change the doodles in this book to make them your own. Don't get discouraged if they don't turn out the way you want the first time—there's a reason pencils come with erasers! Just give it another try, and have fun.

Your friends at American Girl

How to Do a Doodle

Doodling is a casual and fun way to draw. If you want to make changes to the doodles you see in this book—great! But if you want your doodles to look just like the ones here, that's OK, too. Whatever your doodling style, these tips will help your drawings turn out the way you like them.

Practice Makes Better

It's good to doodle lightly in pencil. If your doodle isn't turning out, you can erase part—or all—of it. Try the same doodle a few times, and you'll probably find that it gets easier to draw. Also, before doodling on a bookmark or card, practice on scratch paper. That way, you'll be a pro when you draw your final one.

Look Closely

There are written instructions for the doodles in this book, but it helps to look closely at the step-by-step drawings, too. Pay attention to the lines that get added at each step. How long are they? Do they curve? Where do they attach to the previous lines?

Finishing Touches

Color brings your doodles to life. For best results, draw the doodle in pencil. Fill in the different sections with marker, letting the ink dry between colors. Then use a fine-point marker to go over all your pencil lines at the end. That way, your colors shouldn't smear.

Animal shelter

♥ parakeet ♥

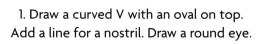

1. Draw a curved V with an oval on top. Add a line for a nostril. Draw a round eye.

2. Draw a long curve for the head and body. Add wings.

3. Draw feet and a perch. Draw a tail. Finish the beak. Add stripes to the wings.

Terrier

1. Draw a scratchy square with two points for the head. Add the back.

2. Draw the tail, back leg, and front leg.

3. Draw the belly, other legs, and a ball. Add the face.

Sleeping Cat

1. Draw a circle with two points for the head.

2. Add a curved back and tail.

3. Draw the face and feet.

Hamster

1. Draw a tall U with a flat bottom.

2. Add ears and feet.

3. Draw a face, front feet, and a tail.

Beagle

1. Draw a diagonal U for the face. Add U's for ears and the tongue.

2. Draw bent loops for the legs.

3. Add the back, tail, face, and a bone.

Turtle

1. Draw three curves.

2. Add a pointed head. Draw two stumpy legs.

3. Draw a pattern on the shell. Add a tail, toes, and a face.

Playful Cat

1. Start with the cat's head. Add a curve on the back, and draw the front leg.

2. Finish the tail and add the back leg. Draw a front leg reaching out.

3. Add a face and a toy mouse.

Bulldog

1. Draw a fat sideways C.
Add a curve underneath.

2. Finish the head with two ears,
eyes, a nose, and a smile.

3. Draw the body. Add feet and a tail.

Sitting Cat

1. Draw the head.
Add a curved back
and a tail.

2. Draw the two
front legs.

3. Add back legs
and the face.

slumber party

♥ sleeping bag & pillow ♥

1. Draw two connected triangles.

2. Add curved lines to the bag. Draw a curved rectangle for the pillow.

3. Draw more curved lines. Add details to the pillow.

teddy bear

1. Draw a bumpy oval. Add a bumpy body.

2. Draw bumpy ears, arms, and an oval on the face.

3. Draw legs. Add a face and heart.

popcorn

1. Draw two curves.

2. Add stripes to the bowl. Add a row of puffs.

3. Add more puffs to the pile. Draw a few scattered kernels.

Pizza

1. Draw a star with lines.

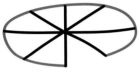

2. Draw an oval around the points.
Draw a triangle.

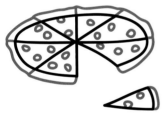

3. Draw a crust and toppings.

Pajamas &
Bunny Slippers

1. Draw a simple
shirt shape.

2. Draw a flower. Add
two long lines and
two clouds.

3. Draw legs. Add
details to shirt,
pants, and slippers.

Toothbrush & Toothpaste

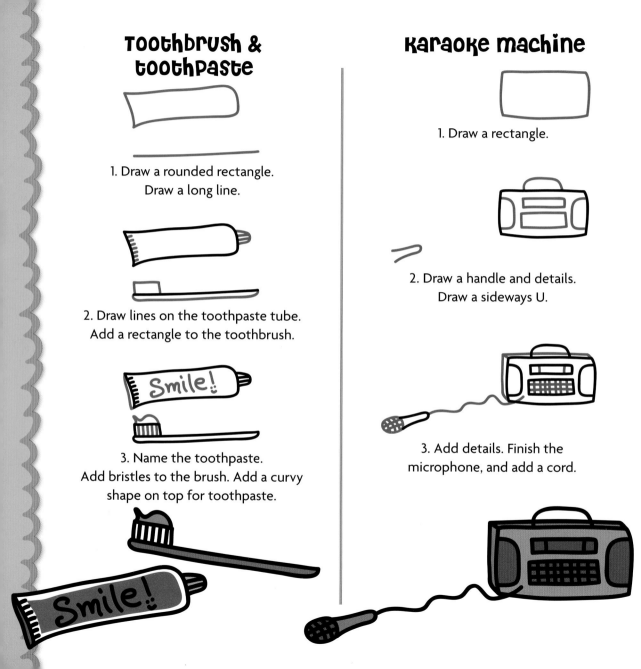

1. Draw a rounded rectangle.
Draw a long line.

2. Draw lines on the toothpaste tube.
Add a rectangle to the toothbrush.

3. Name the toothpaste.
Add bristles to the brush. Add a curvy
shape on top for toothpaste.

Karaoke Machine

1. Draw a rectangle.

2. Draw a handle and details.
Draw a sideways U.

3. Add details. Finish the
microphone, and add a cord.

Smile!

TV

1. Draw two rectangles. Add two curves underneath.

2. Draw a small rectangle with dots. Draw a TV show.

3. Add details to the base, remote control, and screen.

PANCAKES

1. Draw an oval with a drippy bottom.

2. Draw two pancakes underneath.

3. Draw a plate, fork, and pat of butter.

city

♥ skyline ♥

1. Draw a line of boxes at different angles.

2. Draw another line of buildings below.

3. Add windows and a moon.

café chairs

1. Draw two ovals. Add side lines.

2. Draw curves for legs.

3. Add another leg to each. Draw loopy backs.

café table

1. Draw a rectangle with a wavy bottom. Add two lines.

2. Draw curves for the legs and cups. Draw a vase. Draw two spirals.

3. Add flower stems, cup handles, and details.

Fountain

1. Draw two curves with spirals at the ends.

2. Draw sides. Draw a straight line across the bottom.

3. Draw stairs. Add droplets of water.

Storefront

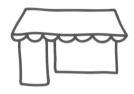

1. Draw a trapezoid. Add a scalloped edge. Draw two rectangles.

2. Draw the walls and roof. Add a sign and stripes. Finish the door.

3. Draw the merchandise, flowerpots, and a welcome mat. Name the store.

Taxicab

1. Draw a long, bending line.

2. Draw bumpers and wheels. Draw a line for the bottom of the cab.

3. Draw windows, doors, lights, and details.

TAXI

Pigeon

1. Draw a long curve. Add a beak.

2. Draw a belly. Add a wing and tail feathers.

3. Draw a face and feet. Add details.

food cart

1. Draw a curve. Draw a rectangle.

2. Draw bumps under the curve. Add boxes, a wheel, and a stand.

3. Add stripes to the umbrella. Draw other details.

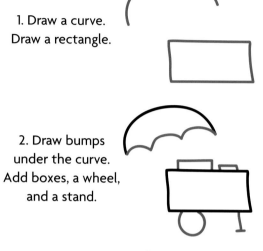

squirrel

1. Draw a pointed curve. Add an ear and a wavy line.

2. Draw a long curve for the tail. Add a squiggly line. Draw an arm and an acorn.

3. Draw a belly and two legs. Add a face.

camping

♥ Raccoon ♥

1. Draw a wide head with ears. Add two wide curves.

2. Draw a mask and feet. Finish the tail. Add a back leg.

3. Draw a face. Add front legs. Draw the belly and other back leg. Add stripes.

BACKPACK

1. Draw an oval with a flat bottom. Add a curve on the side.

2. Draw a spiral, a zipper, and a pocket.

3. Draw curves to finish the sleeping mat. Add straps.

TOASTY MARSHMALLOW

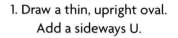

1. Draw a thin, upright oval. Add a sideways U.

2. Add a long, thin stick. Draw a point on the side of the marshmallow.

3. Draw a line for a twig. Add a leaf.

pine tree

1. Draw an upside-down V. Add curvy points.

2. Draw two more layers of curvy points.

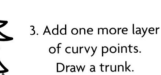

3. Add one more layer of curvy points. Draw a trunk.

moon

1. Draw a pointed curve.

2. Draw two flat clouds.

3. Add a curve to finish the moon. Draw two stars.

mountains

1. Draw a pointed curve. Add another.

2. Draw a wiggly line on each for snow.

3. Draw a sun and birds.

owl

1. Draw a tall U.

2. Close the top with points. Add two circles, a triangle, and two curves.

3. Add dots, stripes, and feet.

Tent

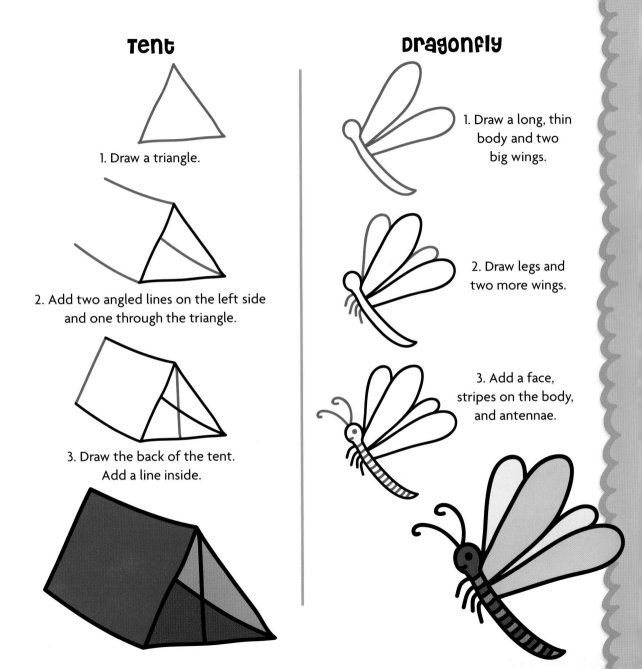

1. Draw a triangle.

2. Add two angled lines on the left side and one through the triangle.

3. Draw the back of the tent. Add a line inside.

Dragonfly

1. Draw a long, thin body and two big wings.

2. Draw legs and two more wings.

3. Add a face, stripes on the body, and antennae.

sporty mice

♥ Basic mouse ♥

1. Draw an oval. Add two curves on top.

2. Draw smaller curves inside the ears. Add dots for a face. Draw lines for arms and legs.

3. Draw rounded hearts for hands and feet. Add a tail and a smile.

pom-pom mouse

1. Draw an upside-down U. Add two ears. Draw a line across the bottom.

2. Draw a skirt. Draw arms. Add a face.

3. Draw two pom-poms. Add legs, feet, a bow, and a tail.

volleyball mouse

1. Draw an oval with an ear.

2. Draw a face and another ear. Draw curved lines for a bikini.

3. Draw arms, legs, and a tail. Draw a ball.

ice-skating mouse

swimming mouse

1. Draw an oval. Add ears.

1. Draw an oval. Add ears.

2. Draw a skirt. Add arms, legs, and a face.

2. Draw arms and hands. Add a curve for the swim cap. Draw the trunks.

3. Draw hands and feet. Add skates and a tail.

3. Draw a face with goggles. Add a tail, flippers, and other details.

soccer mouse

1. Draw an oval. Add ears and a face.

2. Add arms, legs, hands, and feet. Draw a line for shorts. Add a tail.

3. Add details to shorts. Draw shin guards and cleats. Draw the ball.

tennis mouse

1. Draw an oval. Add ears and a face.

2. Draw a skirt. Draw arms, legs, hands, feet, and a tail.

3. Draw two curves for the sweatband. Add a racket and ball.

Skiing Mouse

1. Draw an oval. Add a helmet, strap, and glasses.

2. Draw ears, a face, arms, legs, hands, and feet. Add a lift ticket.

3. Draw skis and poles.

Softball Mouse

1. Draw a sideways oval for a brim. Draw the cap, ears, and body.

2. Draw a face, arms, legs, feet, a hand, and a mitt.

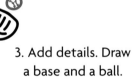

3. Add details. Draw a base and a ball.

football mouse

1. Draw a mouse body with helmet shape. Add an ear.

2. Draw arms and hands. Add a face, face mask, and another ear. Draw a ball.

3. Draw legs, feet, and a tail. Add stripes. Add details to the ball.

Basketball mouse

1. Draw an oval. Add ears. Draw arms and legs.

2. Draw hands and feet. Add a face. Draw two curves for a sweatband.

3. Draw a curve for the jersey. Add a tail, a ball, and other details.

Gymnast mouse

1. Draw an oval. Add ears.

2. Draw a face. Add legs and feet. Draw a long rectangle.

3. Draw arms, hands, tail, and leotard line. Finish the beam.

Skateboarding mouse

1. Draw a helmet. Draw the body underneath.

2. Draw ears, arms, and legs. Draw an oval underneath.

3. Draw a face, safety pads, and other details.

sweets

♥ fancy cake ♥

1. Draw the bottom layer first. Add two more layers on top.

2. Draw a straight line with scallops for the base. Add two curls.

3. Draw a heart on top. Add loops and dots and other details.

ice-cream cone

1. Draw a wide upside-down U. Add a squiggle underneath.

2. Draw two more scoops. Add a V for the cone.

3. Draw a cherry and other details.

cookies & milk

1. Draw a bumpy oval. Draw a thin oval with two lines down the sides.

2. Draw four more cookies. Draw a thin oval inside the glass. Finish the bottom. Add two lines.

3. Draw a plate. Add chocolate chips and finish the napkin.

BANANA SPLIT

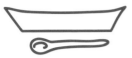

1. Draw a dish with straight sides and a spoon.

2. Draw two curves for bananas. Add three scoops. Draw clouds on top.

3. Draw cherries, sauce, whipped cream, and other details.

CUPCAKE

1. Draw two slanted lines. Connect them at the bottom with a straight line.

2. Draw a cloud on top.

3. Draw a cherry. Add sprinkles and stripes.

candy apple

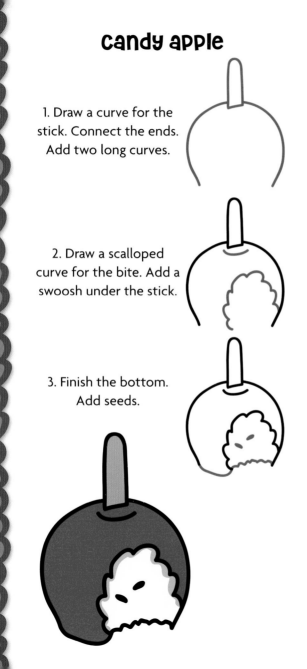

1. Draw a curve for the stick. Connect the ends. Add two long curves.

2. Draw a scalloped curve for the bite. Add a swoosh under the stick.

3. Finish the bottom. Add seeds.

cake slice

1. Draw a triangle. Draw two lines down from the corners.

2. Draw the cake layers. Add frosting.

3. Draw a spiral with a leaf for the flower. Add a plate.

DONUT

1. Draw a wide oval.

2. Draw a smaller oval. Add a curved, squiggly line.

3. Draw a curve inside the donut hole. Add sprinkles.

BOX OF DONUTS

1. Draw a rectangle. Add three upside-down U's on top.

2. Draw two lines off the side. Add another row of upside-down U's.

3. Draw the lid and the side. Add donut holes and other details.

♥ firefly ♥

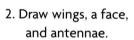

1. Draw three ovals to make the body.

2. Draw wings, a face, and antennae.

3. Add more wings and legs.

Birdbath

1. Draw an oval. Add sides. Draw two bird shapes.

2. Draw a wavy line. Add the base.

3. Draw grass and water. Finish the birds.

Birdhouse

1. Draw a house shape. Add a bird head and a roof line.

2. Draw the rest of the roof, the side, and house details. Add a branch.

3. Draw leaves on the branch and wavy lines on the roof.

sunflower

1. Draw an oval.

2. Draw petals, a stem, and grass.

3. Draw leaves and dots.

Garden gnome

1. Draw a triangle. Add a wobbly triangle underneath.

2. Draw arms and hands. Add the body. Make a curve for the top of the beard. Draw a line in one hand.

3. Draw legs and boots. Finish the shovel. Draw the face.

Toadstool

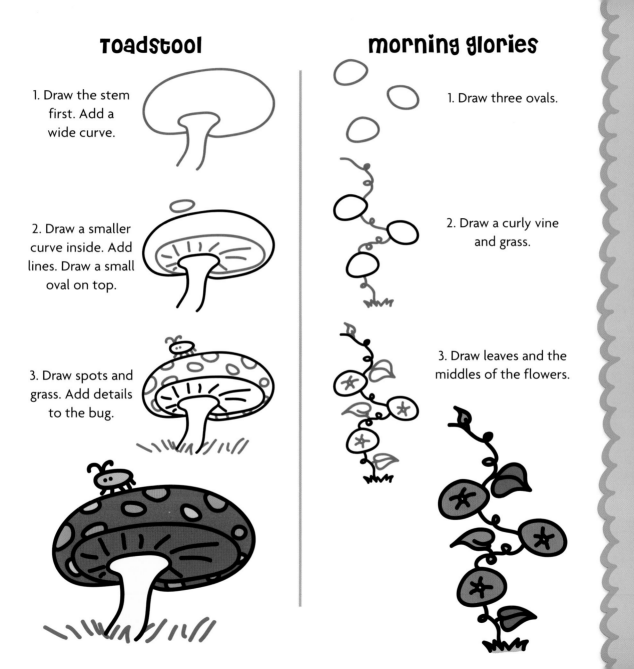

1. Draw the stem first. Add a wide curve.

2. Draw a smaller curve inside. Add lines. Draw a small oval on top.

3. Draw spots and grass. Add details to the bug.

morning glories

1. Draw three ovals.

2. Draw a curly vine and grass.

3. Draw leaves and the middles of the flowers.

Frog

1. Draw a big curve and two small curves.

2. Draw legs. Add the bottom line.

3. Draw arms. Add a face.

Tulips

1. Draw two curly lines. Add a rounded triangle inside each.

2. Draw the petals, stems, and leaves.

3. Add ground, more leaves, and details.

shoes

♥ clogs ♥

1. Draw two big curves. Add two smaller curves.

2. Draw two even smaller curves.

3. Draw the soles. Add flowers.

Flip-Flops

1. Draw two bent ovals.

2. Draw straps. Add a curve at the bottom of each shoe.

3. Draw stripes.

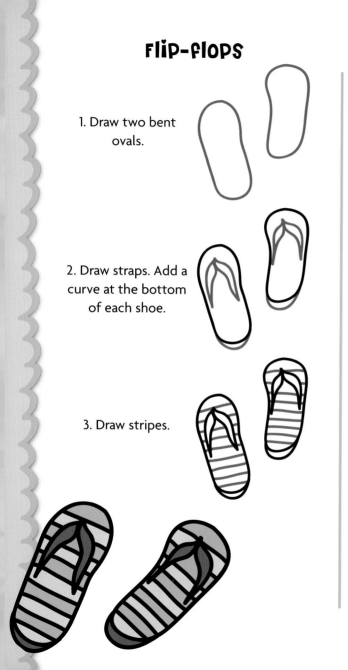

Cowboy Boots

1. Draw bent lines. Follow shapes closely.

2. Draw soles and heels. Finish tops of boots.

3. Draw details and decorations.

Mary Janes

1. Draw two ovals with straps across.

2. Draw two curving lines for the bodies of the shoes.

3. Draw soles, inside lines, and a snap.

Rain boots

1. Draw two thin ovals. Add a curving line.

2. Draw two curves for the fronts of the boots.

3. Add soles and loops. Add flowers.

Fuzzy boots

1. Draw a bent curve. Add another bent line.

2. Draw puffs at the top. Add soles.

3. Draw tassels and other details.

Ballet flats

1. Draw a bent oval and a curve.

2. Draw two curves and a heel.

3. Add the bows and inside line.

sandals

1. Draw two curving lines.
Add two short vertical lines.

2. Draw the heels. Draw straps. Add curves.

3. Draw ovals for the ankle straps. Add buckles.

write to us

1. Make up your own doodle.

2. Sign it and put it in an envelope.

3. Mail it to
Scribble, Squiggle & Sketch Editor
American Girl
8400 Fairway Place
Middleton, WI 53562

Sorry, doodles can't be returned. All comments and suggestions received by American Girl may be used without compensation or acknowledgment.

Here are some other American Girl books you might like:

❏ I read it.

❏ I read it.

❏ I read it.

❏ I read it.

❏ I read it.